HANDBOOK OF PYTHON

RAMPRAKASH S

My Father Thiru "R.Singaravel"

My Mother Thirumathi "S.Chandra"

&

My Wife Mrs.S.Uma Mageshwari

Contents

Preface

This book depicts the basics of python which is very useful for beginners and those who are all willing to learn and coding in python. Nowadays python plays a major role in the industrial and programming environment, and most industries need python programmers to develop many applications like web development, mobile app development, etc., This book definitely helps for the age group of 10 to anyone., Easy examples are given in each and every chapter that is very easy to understand for user needs.

- **Ramprakash S**

Acknowledgements

My Brother Thiru.S.Saravana Prakash
    Dean Dr.M.Durairasan (UCE, Thirukkuvalai)
    Department of CSE Staffs (UCE Thirukkuvalai)
    My Dear Friends & Relatives
    &
    Finally
    Guido Van Rossum (Founder of Python)

CHAPTER ONE

Introduction to Python

Python is open-source programming. Nowadays in the industry concern, it plays a major role. According to recent surveys, python is the best and first among all programming languages. Python is used different platforms such as machine learning, statistical analysis, Deep Learning, etc.,

Python is a high-level programming language, that can be understandable by both machines and human beings. It has a variety of sub-fields like Data Structures using python, Object Oriented Programming using Python-like we are using in C and C++ programming languages., of course, the basics of python is derived from 'C' programming language only which means the fundamental of Python is to know the concept of the 'C' programming language.

By using Python

- The amount of Programming coding is very less , so memory space must be reduced.
- Time can be minimized.
- Flexible to write the codings.

Python Installation

Python versions 2.x and 3.x can be installed manually. But nowadays python version 3.x is preferable. Python installation of Windows, Linux, and Mac operating systems is supported. Though it is an open-source programming language so, there is no need to pay any amount of download. You can download it free of cost.

Steps to Install Python in Windows OS:

- Go to www.python.org website page.
- Under the "Downloads" menu select Windows OS
- Select the latest version of Python (e.x Python 3.9.6)
- After Downloading, select the python folder extract, and install it.
- Next->Next>Finish it
- Now Python GUI window will open.
- >>> symbol shows you can successfully installed Python.

Linux OS Installation:

- Go to www.python.org website page.
- Under the "Downloads" menu select Others OS
- Select the latest version of Python (e.x Python 3.9.6)
- After Downloading, select the tar.xz folder extract and install it.
- Go to terminal go the folder where your tar folder of python is located
- give the command tar xvf python.x.tar.xz folder
- untar and configure -> make the file

- >>> symbol shows you can successfully installed Python.

After the installation in windows and Linux and mac os, the desired command prompt mode will be displayed.it starts with >>> symbol. Python GUI IDLE (Graphical User Interface Integrated Development Environment) will be open in Command Prompt mode. In Command Prompt top menu go to File-> New->New Script.py will be open .,You can type the script and save the file extension is .PY extension and RUN the Program in RUN Menu.

In the python command, the prompt >>> symbol shows the python interpreter symbol to tell the python environment is.

First Program

When we add two numbers in python just give the command
>>>5+3
>>>8 will be
returned as answer.,

>>>5%3
>>>2 will be the answer here python will be very simple when compared with other programming languages. In 'C'Program language it has a structure like

```
#include<stdio.h>
#include<conio.h>
void main()
```

```
{
int a, b,c;
printf("enter the two numbers");
scanf("%d%d",&a,&b);
c=a+b;
printf("The addition of two numbers is %d", c);
getch();
}
```

which returns addition of two numbers it will take more than 10 lines of code, but python will take only one line or maximum two lines of code.,so where both memory and timing constraint have been reduced.

Print the statements

In python printing of statements take very lesser space.,using print keyword it will be print any statement as
>>>print("Hi welcome to Python Programming")
>>>Hi Welcome to Python Programming
it will be print as same as what we are given input to the python prompt.
By using Variable in python is store any value and print the value
>>>a=98+65
>>>a
it gives the answer of
>>>163

INPUT Keyword in Python:
Another input of python is to give the keyword of input ,its look like scanf in "C" Programming language.,initialize any variable with input is like
>>>a=input("enter the value")

>>>enter the value

will be the output when will have values give it will get desired output.

CHAPTER TWO

Types in Python

There are different types of data in python which can differ from other programming languages. Normally data type is to identify the type of data in any programming languages.In 'C" Programming language it refers to "data type" like integer, character, double, long double, the float is used., Only the difference is Character data type is not supported in python., In python type of data, id identify by the "type " keyword.

Integer - Integers are whole numbers which can be start from negative numbers to positive numbers.,(e.x) -723 , 10, -10,18

In Python command prompt will run the following examples return "int" type

Integer

```
    >>>type(-567)
>>>---int----
>>>a=12
>>>type(a)
>>>---int----
>>>a=-8765
>>>type(a)
>>>----int----
```

Float - It displays the whole fractional numbers with point representation.

>>>type(-89.17)

>>>--float--

>>>f=90.67

>>>type(f)

>>>--float---

>>>p=3.14

>>>type(p)

>>>--float---

String - It is defined as the collection of characters with single-quoted or Double quoted.

>>>type("hi welcome to python")

>>>--str--- here Str displays string type

>>>a="welcome"

>>>type(a)

>>>---str---

Complex - Which is the mathematical function consists of the Real and imaginary part.,

>>>type(1+1j)

>>>--complex---

>>>a=3+9j

>>>type(a)

>>>--complex--

Boolean - Which returns either True or False for the conditional statements.

>>>1==1

>>>---True---

>>>2!=2

>>>---False--- alaways boolean statements return True or False value where "T' and "F' are Uppercase letter.

None Type - Which returns Null value or Empty value.,

>>>type(None) ---> Null value represented

CHAPTER THREE

Numbers Representation

Numbers representation in python is similar to number systems used in digital namely Binary, Octal, Hexadecimal representation. In python Binary representation starts with '0b' (Zero lower case letter 'b'), Octal representation starts with '0o'(Zero lower case letter 'o'), Hexadecimal representation starts with 'Ox' (Zero followed by lower case letter x).

Binary Representation - Binary Number can be either '0's or 1's

```
>>>print(0b0)
>>>0

>>>print(0b1)
>>>1
```

Octal Representation - Octal number system with the base of 8 supports python.
```
>>>print(0o11)
>>>9
```

>>>print(0o100)
>>>100 wiil be the output

Hexadecimal Representation - Decimal numbers with a-f Characters represent hexadecimal representation with the base of 15 digits.

>>>print(0xa)
>>>10

>>>print(0xf)
>>>15

>>>print(0x67)
>>>103

"Separator" command - Collection of characters are called Strings that have been separated by the keyword "sep" in python.

>>>print("hi","welcome","to","Python
Programming",sep="@")
>>>hi@welcome@to@Python Programming

will be the output where each string separated by @ symbol.

"end" command - each statement of strings have been ending in sequence (means-"end" keyword gives the output in sequence)

>>>print("hi", "welcome","python",end="/")

>>>hi welcome python/

CHAPTER FOUR

Operators in Python

Python supports a variety of operators like arithmetic operators, conditional operators, Logical Operators, Assignment Operators, etc., Arithmetic operators like '+' denotes addition, '-' denotes subtraction, '/' denotes division, '%' denotes modulo which returns the remainder value of the division operation, '//' denotes integer division which returns quotient value which doesn't return any fractional values, meanwhile '/' returns a float quotient value.'*'*, denotes exponential operator and '*' (single star) denotes multiplication...

In python
>>>89+63 -----> Addition Operator

>>>152

>>>65-63 -----> Subrtraction Operator
>>>2

>>>6%5 -----> Division Operator
>>>1

>>>6/5 -----> Division Operator

>>>1.2

>>>17//4 -----> " integer Division Operator
>>>4

>>>6*7 -----> Multiplication Operator
>>>42

>>>3**2 ------> " Exponential" operator
>>>9

Logical Operators like Logical ' and' -& , Logical 'or' - | , 'not' operators ! are used.

>>> 1 and 2
>>>2 ------> it will take two inputs
>>> 2 or 5 ------> it will take any one of the inputs
>>> not 5 -------> The value is not is eual to 5

Conditional operators like < ,> ,<=, >= ,== are denotes in Python
>>>7<6
>>>True

>>>7>5
>>>True

>>>8<=9
>>>True

>>>15>=876
>>>False

>>>98==97
>>>False

>>>9==9
>>>True

Like different types of operators used in python.

CHAPTER FIVE

Evaluation of Arithmetic expressions in Python

Evaluating the arithmetic operations in python starts with the Left to Right way, except for the exponential operator which is evaluated from Right to Left, all other operators supported from left to right. This evaluation based on "PEMDAS" Manner. Meaning of **PEMDAS** is P-Parenthesis, E-Exponential, D-Division, M- Multiplication, A-Addition, S-Subtraction. The evaluation must be left to right.

|- 5

(e.x) *Evalute (5/3)**2/2*5+3-2 ---->6*

| | | |_4

1 2 3

|

---> Parenthesis evaluated (5/3) is---->
1.6666666666666667**2

-----> exponential operation

----->2.777777777777778/2

------> Division Operation

------> 1.38888888888889

-------> Multiply by 5

---------> 6.9444444444455

----------> Addition with 3

-----------> 9.944444444455

------------> Subtarct with 2

Answer ---> 7.94444444445

CHAPTER SIX

Variable , Strings , Swapping in Python

Variable refers to a value that can be changed during the execution of a program. Variable can store the value that can be used for later.

In python, the left-hand side always defines a variable with its corresponding value stored on the right-hand side. examples

```
>>>a=10
>>>print(a) ---------> here 'a ' is avariable which can store
the value of 10
>>>10
```

```
>>>One =1
>>>Two=2
>>>Thirtythree=33
>>>print(One+Two+Thirtythree)
>>>36
```

here the variable stored value have been added which gives the value of 36 as answer.

Memory Allocation

Variable is to store the value means the address of the memory value to be indicated by the keyword "id".Both numbers and strings can give its addresses.,

>>>id(7)
>>>1587124 ----> memory address value of the integer 7 is displayed.

>>>id("ram")
>>>1543181971115551 ----> memory address value of the string "ram" is displayed.

if both the values of the id are the same, it returns the same memory address value. example
>>>a=b=10
>>> id(a)
9785184
> id(b)
9785184
In the above code variable, a and b are initialized to 10, so it returns the same memory id value output.

Strings
Character in 'C' Programming language is replaced by Strings in Python.
>>>a='python'
>>>b='programming'
>>>a+b
>>>'pythonprogramming

Two strings have been concatenated or joining in python

>>>a="hi"+2+"how are you"

>>>print(a)

>>>error will be identified because of 2 can be the integer it cant be converted into a string, so we must put str before 2, now

>>>a="hi"+str(2)+"how are you"

>>>print(a)

>>>'hi2howareyou' ----> displayed

String operations

Split: Splitting of strings done in python.

>>>a="hello python"

>>>a=a.split(" ")[0]

>>>print(a)

>>>hello ----------------> here 0th element splitted and displayed. and 1st element is python,.

Strings Sorted

>>>sorted(['a','A','1'])

>>>['1','A','a'] ------------------------> printed here it will take numbers first, Uppercase letter second, Lowercase letters third to print

>>>sorted(["B","A","S","T")

>>>["A","B","S","T") --------------------------> will be printed

>>>sorted(['a','b','A','G','H','I','1','34'])

>>>['1','34','A','G','H','a','b']

Swapping in Python - In Python two values is to be exchanged by two values without giving swap function

(e.x)
>>>a=10
>>>b=14
>>>a,b=b,a -------> here a and b value have been changed
just giving this statement
>>>print(a)
>>>print(b)
>>>14 value of a= 14
>>>10 value of b=10 is changed

Type Casting in Python

Type is explicitly expressed in python like

integer can take only whole numbers like

>>>int(4.5)
>>>4

>>>int(-100.9)
>>>-100

float will take fractional values

>>>float(8)
>>>8.0

>>>float(23.9)
>>>23.9

CHAPTER SEVEN

Sets, Tuples, Dicitionary in Python

Set- It is a collection of order of elements with open and close braces.

>>>a={2,4,5,6,9,11}
>>>type(a)
>>>set -----------> while giving type it displays set type
   Set operations:

Addition: The addition of two sets can be joining of two sets
>>>a={1,2,3,4}
>>>b={2,3,4}
>>>a|b
>>>{1,2,3,4}

Subtraction :The set subtraction A−B consists of elements that are in A but not in B
>>>a={1,2,3,4,5,6}
>>>b={34,5,6,1,45,67}
>>>a-b
>>>{2, 3, 4}

Intersection: The common element in the set is identified in intersection operation by & opearator.

>>>>>>a={1,2,3,4}
>>>b={2,3,4}
>>>a&b
>>>{2,3,4}

vice versa many more set operations have been identified.

Tuples - It is used to store multiple elements in a single variable with enclosed with open and close brackets.

>>>j=("orange","apple","banana")
>>>type(j)
>>>Tuple

Note :we can't add any element in tuple and set , so its unmutable , meanwhile List is mutable
means we can add the elements in LIST

e.x
>>>j=("orange","apple","banana")
>>>j[0]="grapes"
>>>j
>>>TypeError :Traceback (most recent call last) <ipython-input-19-2e35333dce07> in <module> 1 j=("orange","apple","banana") ----> 2 j[0]="grapes" 3 j TypeError: 'tuple' object does not support item assignment

Tuples - It is used to store multiple elements in a single variable with enclosed with open and close brackets.

```
>>>j=("orange","apple","banana")
>>>type(j)
>>>Tuple
```

Dictionary- It is a collection of unordered elements consists of each key and its values enclosed with its set.

```
>>n={"x1":"car", "x2":"bike","x3":"bus"}
>>>print(n)
>>>{'x1': 'car', 'x2': 'bike', 'x3': 'bus'}
>>>type(n)
>>>dict
```

Membership , Identity operators in python

Membership Operators -In python, the operators in and not in operators are identified by membership operators, here both the operators return boolean values. example to check whether the values are present or not present by the given examples tell the membership operators.

```
>>>a={1,3,5,7,9}
>>>print( 3 in a) -------------> where the value 3 is in
```
variable a, so it returns true value
```
>>>True
```

```
>>>i={12,3,4}
>>>print( 12 not in i} ----------> Where the value 12 is
```
present but not 12 means not present , so it displays False value
```
>>>False
```

Identity Operators - Python supports is and is not display identity operators.

"is" and "is not" -an operator which returns True if the value exists in a sequence or not in the python.

```
>>> 5 is 5
>>>True
```

```
>>> 5 is not 5
>>>False ----> In both statements literally shows warning
```
and returns boolean values

PASS in python - Python supports PASS statement which doesn't return anything., it just pass the value.,
```
sequence = {'p', 'a', 's', 's'}
for val in sequence:
pass
```
where "pass" statement just a statement which doesn't do anything.,

CHAPTER EIGHT

List in python

List is a collection of values enclosed with square brackets. It consists of strings and numbers representation. To define a list it starts with a variable with a list of values to be defined. example

```
>>>a=["hi","welcome","to","python","class"]
>>>print(a)
>>>['hi','welcome','to','python','class']
```

where it displays a value with square brackets to identify the type we just check
```
>>>type(a)
>>>list
```
will be displayed.

Items in the list can be stored the value in index (sequence manner like arrays which starts from 0,1,2,3,,,,,n it can be stored) .,e.x

```
>>>s=['a','b','c','d','e','f']
>>>print(s[0])
>>>a like wise s[1]=b
s[2]=c
```

s[3]=d

s[4]=e

s[5]=f will be displayed.

List Slicing - List can be sliced from Left to Right or Right to Left means cutting the value in both the sides with the index size.

Syntax:

list_variable[start value:end value:step]

(e.x)

>>>d=[1,2,3,4,5,6,7]

>>>print(d[3:6]) -----------> starts with d[3] item to d[6-1]=> d[5] value

>>>['4','5','6'] d[3] =4 to d[5]=6 displayed

always start value to end value-1 is displayed.

negative index value starts with Right most value to Let most value represented.

like

>>>print(d[-1])

>>> 7 for the above example Right hand value starts with 7,6,5,4,3,2,1

>>>print(d[-5])

>>>3

slicing of negative values can be

>>>print(d[-5:-3])

>>>['3','4']

>>>print(d[-7:])

>>>[1,2,3,4,5,6,7] -----------> here it prints the value -7 location to till final value.,(i.e) -7 location starts with 1 with

till 7 printed.

>>>print(d[-7:-1:2])
>>>[1,3,5] ------------> start value with memory location -7
is 1 with 2 step movement 3,5 printed,
[Note : You can exclude the value of -1 location thats 1]

List Operations -List has many operations like append,
insert, remove, to find the length, pop an item, to sort the
value using sort, will discuss one by one.

To define a list
a=["hi","welcome","to","python"]
   len - its used to find the length of the string, how many
elements in the list have been identified.
   >>>len(a)
>>>4
   append - used to add the string at the end in a list.
   >>>a.append(hello)
>>>print(a)
>>>a=["hi","welcome","to","python","hello"] ---> here hello
is added at the end.
   Insert- Insert an element in the list after position is
given.
   >>>a.insert(3,"inserted here") ------------> here at the
position 3, "inserted here" string have been inserted
>>>print(a)
>>>a=["hi","welcome","to","inserted here",python","hello"]
-------->3rd position changed here.
   sort -arrangement of element in ascending order or
descending order denoted here.

>>>v=[23,12,1,3,4,2]

>>>v.sort()

>>>print(v)

>>>[1,2,3,4,12,23] -----------> here above list have been sorted using ascending order.

remove- remove an element from the list

>>>v=[12,3,4,5,6]

>>>v.remove(12)

>>>print(v)

>>>[3,4,5,6] ------------> here the value 12 are removed.

pop- it can remove the top of the element like stack data structure.,

>>>v=[12,3,4,5,6]

>>>v.pop()

>>>print(v)

>>>[12,3,4,5] ---here 6 can be deleted because its the top of the element, likewise different types of list manipulation supported by python.

CHAPTER NINE

Functions in Python

The function is defined as a group of statements that have some specific task to do. The defined function is to be reused later.

In python, the function starts with a keyword def followed by function_name with a list of arguments ended with a colon symbol. The function ends with a return statement.

Syntax:
def function_name():
<statement>
return
function_name()

(e.x) >>>def python():
>>> a=10
>>> print(a)
python() ------------------------------> which calls the
function python here.
>>> 10

In function calling an argument also give a result of any operation in python.

suppose of multiplication of two numbers by using the

function can be expressed as

```
>>> def mul(a,b): <------- |
>>> c=a*b |
>>> print(c) |
>>>   mul(67,32)-----------|  here  mul(67,32)  calls  the
```
function mul(a,b) which multiply 67 and 32 and store it in
c
```
>>> 2144
```

In "C" programming local variable, a global variable defined
in a function is also supported in python function.,The
variable which is defined in the main function is the local
variable that gets priority when compared to a global
variable that is defined outside of the function.
(e.x)
```
>>> def fn():
a=10 ------------> local variable
print(a)
>>>b=24 -----------------------> global variable
>>>fn()
>>>print(b)
>>>10
```
>>>24 It prints local variable first , then only global variable
printed

CHAPTER TEN

Conditional , Looping statements in Python

if statement in python denotes the conditional statement which has a simpler structure when compared to 'c' programming language.

syntax:
if <condition>:
<stmt1>
else:
<stmt2>

(e.x)
>>>a=15
>>> if a>10:
>>> print("True")
>>>else:
print("False")
After writing your code save the file in .py and run the code you will get
>>>True ----------------> In the code 15 is greater than 10 so the condition is true, so it will print True

Nested-if-else:

if <condition>:

<stmt1>

elif<condition>:

<stmt2>

else:

<stmt3>

(e.x)

>>>a=10

>>>b=24

if a>b:

print(" a is greater than b")

elif a<b:

print(" a is less than b")

else:

print(" a is equal to b")

output:

" a is less than b"

Looping statements:

Repetition of statements in python can be carried out by looping function especially while loop in python.

While loop:

while <expression>:

<stmt>

(e.x)

a=30

while a>20:

print(a)

a=a+1

output:

30

31

32

33.....................................goes on it will increment the value

For loop - used to express the value with specific range using 'in' operator

(e.x) a=["hi","hello"]

for item in a:

print(a)

   >>>['hi','hello'] printed

for i in range(10):

print(i) ------------------> range(start,end,step)---> range value always start from 0 to n-1

>>>0,1,2,3,4,5,6,7,8,9 ----------------> range(10)---> prints 0,1,2,,,,,,till 9

also break and continue stemants also supported in python.,

CHAPTER ELEVEN

Advanced functions

import is a keyword in python which import the different types of packages in python.,

*Math - i*mport mathematical functions like to find the log, sin, cos trigonometry values, floor, ceil have been found in python.

>>>import math
>>>print(math.log(10)
>>>2.302585092994046

>>>import math
>>>print(math.sin(90))
>>>print(math.ceil(14.87))
>>>0.8939966636005579 ------------> sin value
>>>15 --> math.ceil to round it to 15 , floor vlaue is 14

re - It imports regular expressions identified by python.

>>>import re
>>>a="HI WELCOME, i am ok"
>>> new =re.sub('[A-Z]',',a) ----------------> here it will destroy UPPERCASE Letters
>>> print(new)
>>>'i am ok' ----------------------> print only lower case letters

instead of [a-z] it will print all UPPERCASE letters,
Numbers can be represented by [0-9], it will print numbers
alone

Matplotlib - it is used to display the graph plots for
visualization

```
>>> import matplotlib.pyplot as plt
>>> plt.plot([1,4,5,6])
>>> plt.show()
```

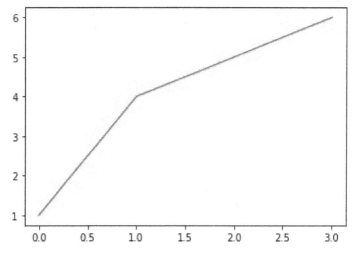

Fig 1: Matplotlib output

Pandas = Python Data Analysis is used to create an
analytical model which is used for statistics

```
import pandas as pd
a=pd.read_csv("copy the path of csv file")
a.describe()
```

(e.x)

```
>>>import pandas as pd
>>>a=pd.read_csv('file:///home/ram/Downloads/
```

melb_data.csv') ----> here CSV file read

\>\>\>a.describe() --------> to show the csv data

This is the output of python pandas csv file

Pandas Output for CSV file

CHAPTER TWELVE

Comments and other functions

Comment in Python is used to identify the description of the coding or program we have to represent in the python platform. It can be denoted with "#"(hash) symbol which means the content is hidden from actual coding.(e.x)

Addition of two numbers ----------------------------> This will tells the description of the program

```
>>>a=13
>>>b=56
>>>c=a+b
>>>print(c)
```

To find the minimum and maximum value in Python

min, max - These are the two important keywords to identify the minimum and maximum values in python.,

min

```
>>>a=min(56,23,15,43,105)
```

```
>>>print(a)
>>>15 -------------> Minimum value is to be printed
```

Max
```
>>>m=max(105,236,596,214,12)
>>>print(m)
>>>596 -----------------> Maximum value is to be printed.
```

CHAPTER THIRTEEN

Hands on Notes -Python

HANDBOOK OF PYTHON

Python Class

Ramprakash

Basic Operations

In [1]:

```
print("hello Welcome to Python Course")
```

hello Welcome to Python Course

In [3]:

```
print(90+63)
```

153

In [4]:

```
print(3.56)
```

3.56

In [5]:

```
4+76
```

Out[5]:

80

In [8]:

```
a=int(input(" enter the vale of a"))
b=int(input("enter the value of b"))
c=a**b   #exponentiation
print(c)
```

 enter the vale of a3
enter the value of b2
9

Data Types in Python"

In [9]:

```
type(89)
```

Out[9]:

int

Hand's on Page 1

In [10]:

```
type("welcome to python Course")
```

Out[10]:

str

In [11]:

```
type(56.26)
```

Out[11]:

float

In [12]:

```
type(4+6j)
```

Out[12]:

complex

In [13]:

```
type(2==3)
```

Out[13]:

bool

In [14]:

```
type(None)
```

Out[14]:

NoneType

Strings # - Collection of characeters enclosed with single quotes or double quotes

In [15]:

```
a="hi"
b="python"
a+b
```

Out[15]:

'hipython'

In [16]:

```
a="python"[0]                #index value start from 0 to n-1 where n is the last el
```

Hand's on Page :2

In [17]:

```
a
```

Out[17]:

```
'p'
```

In [24]:

```
one=23
two=67
print(one+two)
```

90

Variable # - Varibale is a value that can be changed during execution of the program

In [25]:

```
a=12
b=98
a/b
```

Out[25]:

0.12244897959183673

In [26]:

```
a=34+90
b=a//4          ##integer division which returns whole value
b
```

Out[26]:

31

In [27]:

```
a=98
b=45
a&b
```

Out[27]:

32

In [28]:

```
id(a) ---------> Identify the memory stored value
```

Out[28]:

9783904

Hand's on Page : 3

In [29]:

```
id("python")------> Value different for strings
```

Out[29]:

140185404141232

List

List a Value that can be ordered enclosed with suare brackets

In [30]:

```
a=[1,2,3,4]
type(a)
```

Out[30]:

list

In [31]:

```
a.append(5)
a
```

Out[31]:

[1, 2, 3, 4, 5]

In [32]:

```
a.pop(2)
```

Out[32]:

3

In [33]:

```
a
```

Out[33]:

[1, 2, 4, 5]

In [34]:

```
a.remove(1)
a
```

Out[34]:

[2, 4, 5]

Hand's on Page : 4

In [36]:

```
a.insert(2,67)--------> insert an element after the position is given
a
```

Out[36]:

```
[2, 4, 67, 5, 3]
```

In [37]:

```
len(a)
```

Out[37]:

```
5
```

In [38]:

```
a.sort()
```

In [39]:

```
a
```

Out[39]:

```
[2, 3, 4, 5, 67]
```

Type *Markdown* and LaTeX: α^2

Set

Set is Collection of Undered elements

In [41]:

```
a={1,2,3}
a
```

Out[41]:

```
{1, 2, 3}
```

In [45]:

```
a={56,48,34}
a
```

Out[45]:

```
{34, 48, 56}
```

Page 5

In [46]:

```
type(a)
```

Out[46]:

set

In [47]:

```
a={1,2,3,4,5,6}
b={34,5,6,1,45,67}
a-b
```

Out[47]:

{2, 3, 4}

In [48]:

```
a&b
```

Out[48]:

{1, 5, 6}

In [49]:

```
a|b
```

Out[49]:

{1, 2, 3, 4, 5, 6, 34, 45, 67}

In [50]:

```
a^b
```

Out[50]:

{2, 3, 4, 34, 45, 67}

In [54]:

```
for num in a:
    print(num)
```

1
2
3
4
5
6

List slicing

HANDBOOK OF PYTHON

In [63]:
```python
a=["hello","how", "are","you"]
```

In [64]:
```python
a
```
Out[64]:
```
['hello', 'how', 'are', 'you']
```

In [65]:
```python
a[1:2]
```
Out[65]:
```
['how']
```

In [66]:
```python
a[-1]
```
Out[66]:
```
'you'
```

In [67]:
```python
a[2:-1]
```
Out[67]:
```
['are']
```

In [68]:
```python
a[1:3:1]
```
Out[68]:
```
['how', 'are']
```

In [69]:
```python
a[-1:4]
```
Out[69]:
```
['you']
```

In [70]:
```python
a[4:-1]
```
Out[70]:
```
[]
```

Page 7

In [71]:

```
a[3:-1:1]
```

Out[71]:

[]

In [72]:

```
a[:]
```

Out[72]:

['hello', 'how', 'are', 'you']

In [73]:

```
a[-1:1]
```

Out[73]:

[]

Tuple

In [74]:

```
s=(12,34,5,6)[2]
```

In [76]:

```
s
```

Out[76]:

5

In [77]:

```
type(s)
```

Out[77]:

int

In [78]:

```
sa=(12,3,4,5)
type(sa)
```

Out[78]:

tuple

Page 8

• 47 •

HANDBOOK OF PYTHON

In [79]:

```
sa[0]
```

Out[79]:

12

In [80]:

```
we cant insert any value so this is called immutable, but list we can insert so that
```

```
-----------------------------------------------------------------
-----
TypeError                                Traceback (most recent call
last)
<ipython-input-80-2b12c33334c5> in <module>
----> 1 sa[0]='hi'

TypeError: 'tuple' object does not support item assignment
```

In [81]:

```
a={"a":14,"b":23,"c":34,"d":"raja"}
a
```

Out[81]:

{'a': 14, 'b': 23, 'c': 34, 'd': 'raja'}

In [82]:

```
type(a)
```

Out[82]:

dict

In [90]:

```
a={"a1":14,"b":23,"c":34,"d":"raja"}
a
```

Out[90]:

{'a1': 14, 'b': 23, 'c': 34, 'd': 'raja'}

functions

In [94]:

```
def function_name():
    a=90
    print(a)
function_name()
```

90

page 9

In [95]:

```
def a(s,r):
    c=s*r
    print(c)
a(12,35)------- argument function
```

420

Looping and Conditional Statements

In [96]:

```
a=10
if a>10:
    print('yes')
else:
    print('no')
```

no

In [102]:

```
a=98
b=98
if a>b:
    print(a)
elif a<b:
    print(b)
else:
    print("a equal to b")
```

a equal to b

In [103]:

```
range(1,10)
```

Out[103]:

range(1, 10)

In [104]:

```
print(range(1,10))
```

range(1, 10)

Page 10

• 49 •